Kunkush

The True Story of a Refugee Cat

by Marne Ventura   illustrated by Beidi Guo

content consultant, Yasmin Saikia, PhD
Professor of History, Hardt-Nickachos Chair in Peace Studies
Arizona State University

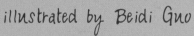

CAPSTONE PRESS
a capstone imprint

The sky was dark. The Aegean Sea splashed against the rubber boat. Men and women huddled together in the cool November air. Most wore life vests. Many held babies and small children.

A widow and her five children were among the families on the boat that night in 2015. They had fled their home in Mosul, Iraq. Islamist State extremists were fighting Iraqi soldiers for control of the city. Tanks and soldiers with guns roamed the streets. Bombs exploded and gunfire rang out all around.

A three-year-old Turkish Van cat named Kunkush crouched in a basket on the widow's lap. The widow and her family had walked for much of the way to Turkey. They couldn't bring their things from home, but they refused to leave Kunkush behind.

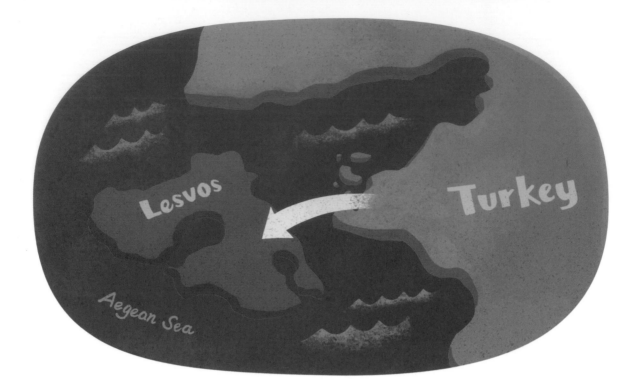

The fighting in Iraq had forced hundreds of thousands to flee. Many went to refugee camps in Turkey. If they could get to Greece, volunteers would help them find new homes in Europe. But to get across the water, they had to pay smugglers to take them secretly during the night.

Kunkush's family had paid an extra 1,000 Euros to bring their cat in a basket.

Crossing the ocean in a rubber raft was dangerous. Often the smugglers let too many people ride at once. Many had drowned when the boats capsized.

Those who made it safely to Greece had more trouble ahead. Camps were overcrowded. Volunteers were running out of supplies. It was becoming harder to find new homes for the refugees. The people on the raft knew about these dangers. They took the risk in hopes of finding better lives.

When Kunkush's boat got near the shore, men jumped off to pull it in. Volunteers rushed out to help. Adults passed crying babies along to safety. Shouts rang out in the darkness. Water splashed everywhere.

Kunkush pushed up the lid of his basket and jumped out. He dashed away through the shallow water. He wanted to be off the boat and away from the chaos. He wanted food and a dry, warm bed.

By the time Kunkush's family was safely
on shore, he was gone.

When the sun came up, Kunkush found himself in a fishing village on the Greek island of Lesvos. His fur, usually white and fluffy, was wet and sandy brown. He was so, so hungry. He didn't recognize the streets or buildings. He couldn't find his family anywhere.

8

Feral cats roamed the village. Local fishers and shop owners put out food for them. Kunkush found some dry cat food scattered on the ground around the patio of a café. He tried to eat, but the other cats bared their teeth, snarled, and jabbed him with sharp claws. He ran away.

Hunger forced Kunkush to come back. But each time, the wild cats chased him off.

Then something good happened. A young woman near the café called out to Kunkush. She was standing next to a car. She had an open can in her hand.

Kunkush ran over and sniffed. Tuna! Fishy, oily tuna!

The feral cats smelled it too. They meowed and ran toward Kunkush.

The young woman opened the car door and motioned for Kunkush to hop in. She got in too. She closed the door, dumped the tuna onto a dish, and set it on the car seat. Then she sat and watched while Kunkush ate.

Kunkush's tail moved from side to side. He licked his paws.

The young woman stroked his head.

He purred.

Kunkush's belly was full when the young woman lifted him out of her car. But the next morning he was hungry again.

Then a second good thing happened.

A volunteer named Amy Shrodes was sitting on the café patio. She was talking to Ashley Anderson, the woman who fed Kunkush in her car. Ashley and Amy had come to Lesvos to help the refugees.

Kunkush pranced over to their table. He meowed and rubbed against Ashley's legs while the women talked.

Amy had noticed Kunkush trying to eat. She could tell he was not a local cat. He wasn't good at fighting for food. He was the only cat with long, white fur. He seemed hungry, dirty, and scared. This was a cat that belonged to a family. A refugee family? Where were they?

Kunkush was getting luckier by the minute.

Ashley and Amy talked about how, with all the sadness around them, they would like to give a refugee family a happy ending. What if they could reunite the cat and his family? They didn't know the family's name. They didn't know the cat's name. They didn't know where the family went. But they were sure the family missed their cat. They decided to try! They would call the cat Dias, the Greek name for Zeus.

Amy asked other volunteers if they knew who owned Kunkush. Two coworkers remembered seeing him run away the night his family arrived. They had helped the family search for several hours to find their cat. Finally they had to give up. It was time for the family to move on to the refugee camp.

On Lesvos, people don't usually keep cats as house pets. But Amy's landlord, Ignatious, loved cats. He was a refugee too. He had come on a boat from Turkey years ago as a boy. When Amy asked if she could keep the cat in her apartment, Ignatious agreed.

Amy took Kunkush to the veterinarian. He got vaccinations.
To check on his health, the vet had to shave Kunkush.

Kunkush looked skinny without his
fur. He was cold. Amy took him home
and gave him a bath. She warmed him
up with dry towels.

She put a little sweater on him.
Then she set him down on a soft
pillow. He was so exhausted from
all the commotion that he fell
asleep on his face.

Amy had a friend named Michelle Nhin who lived in Oklahoma. Michelle was a volunteer like Amy. She had experience using social media. When Amy and Ashley asked Michelle to help them find Kunkush's family, she agreed.

The women created a Facebook page named *Reunite Dias*. They posted Kunkush's story and asked everyone to share it. If they could tell enough people about Kunkush, maybe they could find his family.

While the women were busy working, Kunkush snuggled with Ignatious. The cat stayed warm in his sweater. He ate the good cat food and treats that Amy gave him.

ICELAND

NORWAY

SWEDEN

FINLAND

RUSSIA

ESTONIA

LATVIA

LITHUANIA

BELARUS

North Sea

DENMARK

IRELAND

GREAT BRITAIN

NETHERLANDS

BELGIUM

LUX.

GERMANY

POLAND

UKRAINE

CZECH REP.

SLOVAKIA

MOLDOVA

HUNGARY

ROMANIA

FRANCE

SWITZERLAND

AUSTRIA

SLOVENIA

CROATIA

BOS. & HER.

SERBIA

BULGARIA

MONT. KOS.

MACEDONIA

ALB.

GREECE

TURKEY

PORTUGAL

SPAIN

ITALY

Mediterranean Sea

A woman named Emma in Germany saw the *Reunite Dias* page. She offered to be Kunkush's foster mother. If the volunteers didn't find the cat's family in one year, she would adopt him.

Amy, Ashley, and Michelle decided this was a good plan. Many refugees from Greece go to Germany. Perhaps they could find Kunkush's family there.

On January 4, 2016, Kunkush crouched inside a little carrier once again. This time it was a crate on Amy's lap. He was silent during the flight from Lesvos to Germany. But once Amy got off the plane he meowed and yelled.

Before long he was in a nice, warm apartment. A new lady picked him up and sat down with him on a big chair. She snuggled him into her lap and stroked his fur. Kunkush closed his eyes and purred.

Kunkush settled in at Emma's. His fur had grown long and fluffy. He had plenty to eat. He had a cat tree for climbing, and a fancy pillow to sit on.

Meanwhile, 4,000 people had shared the *Reunite Dias* page. Newspapers, and television and radio stations were also putting out the story of the lost cat.

By now, Kunkush's family had settled in Norway. On February 12, 2016, they read some good news in a British online newspaper, the *Daily Mail*. The same day, they heard the same news on a Norwegian television station.

The family was elated! Someone had found their cat!

On Valentine's Day, the family contacted the *Reunite Dias* team. With the help of their neighbors, they set up a video chat between the family in Norway, the cat in Berlin, and the volunteers. The family crowded around the monitor and cried out with joy when they saw Kunkush.

The volunteers also thought that Kunkush recognized his family.

But Kunkush was confused by the video chat. He kept looking behind the computer to find them!

Next Kunkush made another friend. Doug Kuntz was a photojournalist who had lived next door to Amy in Greece. He offered to fly with Kunkush from Germany to Norway.

The *Reunite Dias* team had done a great job of spreading Kunkush's story. When Doug and Kunkush got off the plane, people recognized them and cheered!

Reporters with cameras were at the family's apartment when Kunkush arrived. Amy watched through a computer videocamera.

Doug ran the doorbell. The door swung open and there was Kunkush's family. The mother started to cry.

"Kunkush! My life!" she cried. She tried to unzip the carrier but it was hard with tears in her eyes.

Doug helped get Kunkush out and into the mother's arms. The mother hugged the cat and buried her face in its soft fur. The whole family gathered around. Now everyone was crying.

Soon Kunkush was purring as he snuggled with his family. In four months, he had traveled 2,000 miles. He had met many kind, generous people. He had ended up right where he belonged. It was a very happy ending.

Happily Ever After

Kunkush was happy in Norway. Amy, Ashley, and Michelle checked up on him regularly through video chats. He was having all kinds of fun with his family. He enjoyed napping, playing with his younger sisters, and watching out the window He got plenty of cuddling. He even liked the snow! Each time they spoke, the family sent their thanks and love to the *Reunite Dias* team for their kindness and generosity. On June 2, 2016, Kunkush passed away unexpectedly from a viral disease. As sad as his passing was, his life was a happy story. Because a few people cared enough to take action, a scared little cat and the family that loved him were reunited.

Glossary

extremist – in politics, a person whose beliefs are very different and out of step with those of most people

feral – wild, not tame

monitor – a video screen on a computer

photojournalist – one who reports news by using photographs

post – on computers, words and pictures that are placed on a website

refugee – a person who escapes from danger to find safety

share – on computers, to make posts available for others to see

smuggler – one who takes something or someone from one place to another secretly and illegally

social media – websites and computer applications that allow people to share information using the Internet

video chat – face-to-face conversations using a computer, the Internet, and a camera

volunteer – a person who does a job for free

Read More

Kent, Deborah. *Middle Eastern Migration*. Minneapolis, Minn.: Capstone, 2012.

Mason, Paul, *Iraq*. Minneapolis, Minn.: Capstone, 2012.

Woolf, Alex. *Let's Think About the Internet and Social Media*. Minneapolis, Minn.: Capstone, 2015.

Internet Sites

Use FactHound to find Internet sites related to this book.

Here's all you do:

Visit www.facthound.com

Just type in 9781515773191 and go.

Write About It!

1. What was Amy and Ashley's plan for reuniting Kunkush with his family? Who did they enlist to help?

2. This book tells the story from Kunkush's vantage point. If his family told the story, what details might they tell differently? What parts of the story would they be unable to tell? What untold parts of the story would they reveal?

3. The *Reunite Dias* team wanted to create a happy ending for the refugee family. Some volunteers criticized them for spending time and energy on a cat when so many people needed help. Do you agree or disagree with this criticism? What are the reasons for your opinion?

Index

Kunkush is published by
Capstone Press, a Capstone imprint
1710 Roe Crest Drive, North Mankato, Minnesota 56003
www.mycapstone.com

Copyright © 2018 Capstone Press

Library of Congress Cataloging-in-Publication Data is available on the Library of Congress website.
978-1-5157-7319-1 (library bound hardcover)
978-1-5157-7331-3 (eBook PDF)

Summary: The true story of a cat separated from, and reunited with, his family
when they fled Iraq for safety.

Editor: Michelle Bisson
Designer: Ashlee Suker

Photo credit: Reunite Dias Team, page 28

Printed and bound in China.
010294F17